Rules for Reluctant Managers

Guidelines for People Who Never Wanted to Be in Charge

Irvin R. Katz, PhD

Purple Breeze Press, LLC

Purple Breeze
PRESS

purplebreezepress.com

Rules for Reluctant Managers: Guidelines for People Who Never Wanted to Be in Charge

Rules for Reluctant Managers: Guidelines for People Who Never Wanted to Be in Charge reflects the author's recollections of experiences over time. Some names and descriptions have been changed. Events have been drawn from memory. Some dialogue has been recreated or reimagined.

Library of Congress Cataloguing in Publication Data
Names: Katz, Irvin R. author
Title: *Rules for Reluctant Managers: Guidelines for People Who Never Wanted to Be in Charge*
Description: First edition. | Purple Breeze Press, 2025
Library of Congress Control Number: 2025917500
ISBN Paperback: 979-8-9918895-4-4

Book designed and copy edited by Meg Vezzu / megvezzu.com

For Ruby, Rick, and Tony.

Everything I know about good management began with you.

Contents

The Reluctant Manager

I never wanted to be a manager. I never thought that I could run things better (OK, a little). I never wanted to climb the corporate ladder; never wanted to have a fancy title or bigger salary. I didn't see my standing defined by the number of people who reported (directly or indirectly) to me. I never expected to manage anyone, let alone be a mid-level manager of over thirty-five employees. Instead, I saw my career as conducting research, supporting others' research through collaboration and mentorship, and helping the business units (the money-making arm of the organization) by applying research results to real-world business needs.

Nevertheless, I found myself as the director of a small group within my organization's Research and Development (R&D) division. I took on the role as a favor to the previous director, who was about to become the senior director of our larger division within R&D. Previously, I had been a research scientist in that group as well as in other areas of R&D. I had no business or managerial training.

Over the next decade, I took on even more management responsibilities, including directing a larger group of scientists and then becoming a senior director of an even larger group of scientists and engineers.

To learn to be a manager, I first spent time reading books on management. These books were rarely helpful. Most of them seemed to assume that their readers wanted to be managers. They didn't give any advice on what to do if you weren't sure you wanted to be in charge—that is, how to behave as a manager if you never even imagined that you'd be in that role someday. And none of them addressed my main concerns about leading a research group—a group consisting of professional scientists who pursue research questions that align with their interests and expertise, the goals of the Research and Development division, and the mission (both business and social) of the organization as a whole.

Instead of relying on books, I began to talk with and observe other managers in my organization and at other research organizations. I began to collect rules for managing—guidelines and strategies for thinking about what it meant to be a manager, the function of a manager, and how to deal with challenges that arose as a manager. As I clarified my thinking about management, when I saw challenges (and solutions), or just when I had a noteworthy interaction with someone, I would add to the list.

This book is a compilation of those rules and the motivations behind them, collected over my years as a manager. I purposely kept the rules short—only two to three sentences—trying to distill the essence of what was a complicated and nuanced situation (or situations). The text accompanying each rule provides context (often given as anecdotes) and the limits of each rule. This list of concrete rules was my secret weapon in dealing with my reluctance and lack of experience.

In some ways, I have been working on this book for fifteen years, starting when I was first asked to be a manager. The book didn't leap fully formed from my head like Athena, although like Zeus, I did often have a headache. When I was first asked to be a director, I learned my first rule ("You WILL make mistakes") and wrote it down in a file I titled "Rules for Management." Over the years, I added to this file when I felt I had learned something new. There were many sources of learning over the years. I learned when I

- successfully navigated a management challenge,
- unsuccessfully navigated a management challenge,
- watched another manager do something I admired,
- watched another manager make mistakes,
- received good guidance from my managers, and
- was treated poorly by my managers.

Only when I was writing this book did I realize that I had been working toward a clear vision of what management meant to me that had guided me over these years. As the "Rules for Management" file got larger (there are still more rules that weren't included in this book), I curated my experiences. Not every success or failure became a rule, just those that seemed "right"—that fit the vision I was building. I gained strength from books such as Susan Cain's *Quiet* that suggested that managers need not be loud and aggressive and from Ken Blanchard and Spencer Johnson's *The One Minute Manager,* which taught me to trust (yet verify) the people in my group. More recently, the descriptions of Bill Campbell's advice in Eagle, Schmidt, and Rosenberg's *Trillion Dollar Coach* confirmed ideas about how management could be an act of building up employees and helping them succeed. Throughout the years, my successes and many failures led me toward an idea of management that could simultaneously be kind and respectful, strong and decisive, and supportive and effective.

A note about the overall business context: The people in my group were primarily scientists; their job functions included thinking about research problems, collecting data to challenge hypotheses, and publishing research findings. During my thirty years at the organization, the research area was more of a think tank than a corporation; there was only indirect concern with the bottom line and no concern with shareholders or market value. Being a researcher was similar to being a university professor, except there was no teaching requirement, the pay was better, and there were more resources for conducting research. Several of the rules in this book refer to the special type of management involved—guiding, mentoring, or coaching highly accomplished scientists. At the same time, in discussions with managers from a variety of for-profit and nonprofit companies, I have learned that these rules apply broadly to reluctant managers everywhere and to situations beyond the conditions in which I learned them.

This context led me to consider writing a book for people who find themselves in a management position but have no prior management experience or expectations. In some organizations, moving from individual contributor to manager is inevitable; there is no career growth without such a move. If you are at such an organization, you will find useful ideas in this book about topics that are rarely discussed in MBA-style management texts, such as persuasion and getting along with peer managers.

There are some important topics that this book does not cover because many other management books address them. In particular, this book will not

- teach you how to deal with toxic situations (everyone at my organization was very pleasant),
- discuss getting ahead in an organization (that wasn't my goal),
- cover productivity situations directly, HR problems, or performance reviews/objectives (all best managed by an HR professional),

- help you in your career other than to teach you how to be a better manager,
- teach you how to directly advocate for your group (I was bad at this, or at least not as aggressive as some of my peer managers), or
- teach you how to get "real" work done (i.e., your projects) while a manager. I never could do this, and it was frustrating because I had been, and preferred to be, an individual contributor to my organization.[1]

About this Book

I have divided the rules into four sections, each addressing key issues in management: Crises, Persuasion, Trust, and Basics. Within each section, I present rules along with a description and illustrative anecdotes inspired by my own and others' real-life experiences. I changed many details of the anecdotes, including the names, genders, and number of individuals involved. The table shows how the rules in each section relate in terms of the timeframe during which they are applied (just once vs. several

1 I have known few people that managed to protect enough of their time to pursue their projects. I do not include managers who assign people in their group to work on their projects. As you will see elsewhere in the book, that approach does not reflect the values of a manager who is helping to build the careers of the professionals in his or her group.

times over a longer period of time) and the specificity of the goal each rule is trying to help you to achieve (a clear, concrete goal, such as to solve an immediate crisis vs. something more abstract or ephemeral, such as building trust).

		Timeframe of Rules	
		Short-Term	Long-Term
Types of Goals	Concrete	**Crises**	**Persuasion**
	Abstract	**Basics**	**Trust**

In the section on crises, I present rules to help you react (or not react) when faced with a problematic situation. Almost by definition, many crises occur suddenly, without warning, and it is amazingly easy for a manager to overreact. My hope is that these rules provide you with some grounding and a basis for making good decisions in a stressful situation. The main lesson of the rules in this section is to react decisively, rather than quickly, by taking the time to understand a crisis and its context.

The section on persuasion discusses key skills that can be used to convince someone—whether your own manager or an employee—to do something. That "something" might be taking a particular course of action, making or reversing a decision, implementing a corporate change that can work in an employee's favor, or even just keeping an employee calm and engaged in the face of challenges. The main lesson of these rules is that persuasion takes time and deliberation, helping people to see the benefits (to them and others) in a course of action or decision.

The section on trust describes rules that help you to build trust with the people you are managing or with your peers. Having trust in others, and others having trust in you, is like putting oil in a motor—everything just runs more smoothly. After all, how can you decisively respond to a crisis if your group does not trust you enough to let you know when something is wrong? How can you persuade someone if there is not mutual trust? As a manager, you need to have the trust of the employees in your group but also the trust of your peer managers and your bosses. Just as with the section on persuasion, the main lesson of these rules is that building trust takes time and effort; it cannot be forced. Like dealing with crises, building trust involves learning and understanding as well as action.

The section on management basics contains rules related to the day-to-day activities of managers:

decision-making, delegation, and communication. The rules in this section help move you towards the abstract goal of keeping your group functioning well. They address the lessons I learned about making management bearable, turning it from something I initially feared into something I could handle. The first rule in this section was the first rule I learned—a recognition that I *will* make mistakes—and counterintuitively, did the most to relieve my initial reluctance.

At the end of each section is a set of questions. The purpose of these questions is to help you to apply the rules to your own management situations: crises to be solved, persuasion you need to undertake, trust you must build, and the day-to-day activities of being a manager. I encourage you to use these questions as writing prompts, whether for bulleted notes or an entry in your management journal. After all, I developed the *Rules for Reluctant Managers* over many years, by writing about my experiences and learning from them. Nevertheless, my experiences and the context for those experiences—within a Research and Development division at a nonprofit organization—are likely to be different from your circumstances. These questions bridge that gap, helping you make the rules your own (and to develop some of your own), and build confidence.

SECTION I: CRISES

When a person comes to you with a problem, for them it is a crisis—something they perceive as stopping them from doing or enjoying their work. The first response of many managers is to try to solve the crisis; other managers always turn the crisis into a problem for the employee to solve (as a learning experience or so that the manager does not have to spend time on it). Yet other managers avoid crises, minimizing or delaying facing the crisis in hopes that it will just resolve on its own. Most effective is something in between high involvement and low (or no) involvement. But how do you decide when, how, and to what extent to get involved?

The rules in this section focus on taking time and gathering information to help you think about and address a crisis. They also show approaches to supporting the person or people in crisis, being highly engaged in the solution while not handling it completely on your own.

RULE 1: Before acting, take a beat. Look at the information again, see if there is more that you need, and make sure that you understand it. This advice is not an excuse for delaying or not acting. However, rather than jumping to action, make sure you know why you are acting and at least minimize the chance that you will need to reverse yourself.

It's easy to jump to a conclusion. It's even easier to jump to the wrong conclusion. There seems to be a premium on coming to a fast decision, one that locks people into a course of action. As a manager, with your decision-making potentially affecting the happiness, productivity, or careers of others, making snap judgments has consequences.

I am not saying that one should never reach a conclusion or spend a long time gathering information before reaching a decision. But take a beat. Do not hear something (or just part of something) and think you know what is going on. Push yourself to ask at least a few questions testing your knowledge of the

- situation ("Are you saying that Person X doesn't like it when Y happens?"),
- frequency ("Does Person X say this every time Y happens?" "How often has Y happened?"), or
- importance ("Has this been going on for a while?" "Is this disrupting Person X's work?" "How does Y change Person X's behavior?").

The following example illustrates this point. I received an email from a fellow director, accusing a researcher in my center of publishing work without acknowledging the contribution of researchers in that director's center. In science, not crediting others' contributions in a published work is a serious breach of professional ethics. However, I had worked with the researcher for many years and knew the individual to be honest and gracious with sharing of credit.

My first reaction was to email the director back, denying the claim or at least casting doubt on the accusation. My second reaction was to tell the director that I would investigate the matter. Certainly I have been on the receiving end of such accusations: "Someone has said that you did X, so could you tell me your side of the story?" and knew how it had felt.

That approach has an underlying presumption of guilt—that is, that the accused must be on the defense. It seems like whoever makes the first claim of hurt gets believed more.

I have learned to strive to be more balanced. Instead, I met with the director to gather more information:

- Who was making the accusation?
- Which paper was under question?
- Were there any other papers where these researchers had shared credit?

The answers from the director, and a review of the papers, suggested that the question of authorship and acknowledgment turned out not to be straightforward in this case. We (the directors) backed off so that the employees could resolve the situation on their own. We each gave the employees in our respective groups some advice (see the next rule), but the resolution came from them.

By taking a beat—seeking more information before acting—we avoided unfounded accusations that would have soured future collaborations and potential consequences that could have affected someone's performance review (and yearly raise).

This rule is also an admonishment to be sure you are listening. As managers, we see many examples of employee behaviors and interactions—more so than our colleagues that are not managers. People are good at seeing patterns and at putting situations or behaviors into categories. Be careful about this tendency. As I said, take a moment, take a beat, and ask a few questions either to find out whether this situation is indeed how you see it or at least to learn the nuances of the situation.

High-level managers might be particularly susceptible to jumping to conclusions. Here's a negative example: During a cross-departmental strategy meeting focused on the implementation of a new communication protocol, the director leading the session invited feedback on how the process was being received. One team member began to express concerns they had heard from people in her group, but before she could finish the thought, the director interrupted and launched into a lengthy monologue. The director spent the next ten minutes explaining how all the information had already been provided and emphasizing that any confusion or difficulties were due to employees not paying enough attention. The director also reiterated the various information that had been communicated, which everyone at the meeting already knew about.

This extended speech, delivered in a frustrated tone and repeating well-known information, effectively shut down further discussion. The director assumed what the feedback from the employees was, and preemptively dismissed any issues, discouraging others at the meeting from voicing their concerns. The meeting, which was intended to surface problems, instead created an environment where my peers and I felt it was safer to stay silent rather than risk being similarly rebuffed.

As a result, the director's self-isolation inadvertently resulted in isolation from the very feedback needed, leaving potential issues unaddressed.

What might have been done instead? After hearing the initial concerns, the director might have taken a moment to ask follow-up questions and really dig into the issue. For example, by saying, "Tell me more about what's going wrong with this process for your team," or "Are these problems happening all the time, or are there particular situations where things are breaking down?" By doing so, the director would have shown genuine interest in what everyone in the area had to say, rather than just assuming an understanding of the situation. This kind of response would have made it clear that the director was there to help solve problems, not dismiss them.

In summary, this rule is not just about listening—it is about showing that you care enough to understand what is really going on. If the director had approached the situation this way, they might have uncovered issues that needed fixing and, just as importantly, shown everyone that their concerns were worth taking seriously.

RULE 2: Co-worker relationships are like butterfly wings: easily torn and impossible to repair. Unless absolutely necessary, do not get directly involved. It will only get worse if you try to fix an interpersonal problem. Instead, coach one or both (separately) about how to handle the situation.

Among all my rules, this one has seemed the most counterintuitive for new managers. As a manager, you want to fix things directly—there's a problem in the team and you want to do the managerial action that's closest to the problem. If two people don't get along, you want to jump in and fix that problem—get the people to talk, facilitate a discussion, get one person to be nicer to the other, etc.

Don't.

Instead of you doing the fixing, this is a case where the employees need to work things out with you in a supporting role.[2]

I'm going to talk about two employees—Alex and Taylor (all the names in this book, except my own, have been changed). Alex was a senior member of the team; Taylor was relatively junior but did have expertise. (Remember, everyone I managed was hired with high levels of education—scientists had PhDs, research assistants had PhDs or master's degrees, and admins had bachelor's or master's

2 Of course, if there is a human resources (HR) issue—abuse or harassment—then you must jump in right away. You must get your HR representative involved and get their advice. But even in that case, you are not handling it yourself—you are bringing in an outside party who hopefully brings experience and an open mind to the issue. That should be another rule: Do not be afraid to get HR involved. If you are wondering whether to get HR involved, it is probably a situation that needs HR.

degrees.) For a particular ongoing project, Alex had a lot more experience than Taylor. However, Taylor felt that Alex was too bossy, without the authority of actually being a boss. Although Alex was more senior, and the project leader, instructions sometimes came across in a way that suggested Alex felt Taylor was an employee rather than a co-worker.

This situation was long-standing, but one of the first "people problems" I addressed as a new manager. I jumped in, speaking directly with Alex, pointing out in very gentle terms that Taylor would appreciate it if Alex would recognize Taylor's expertise.

Big mistake.

Alex became overly formal with Taylor, wary of stepping on toes, and the relationship became strained almost immediately. Suddenly Alex didn't know how to talk with Taylor and Taylor didn't know how to talk with Alex. My intervention, however gentle, made matters worse. Perhaps a more skilled person could have talked with Alex, or them both, more effectively. However, not all managers are skilled in this way. Certainly, I wasn't.

I tried a different approach. I mentored Taylor on how to interact and handle interactions with Alex. I wasn't victim-blaming and saying Taylor was at fault. I instead wanted a way to stay out of the situation directly yet still help. I talked with Taylor about their feelings, thinking through the types of behaviors desired (and undesired) from Alex, and figuring out strategies for reducing the undesired behaviors (and how to react when they occur) and increasing the desired behaviors (e.g., more respectful discourse). Instead of being a direct problem solver, I took the role of coach or mentor. Alex didn't see a problem, so addressing a "problem" would make no sense. Instead, I focused on the person who perceived the problem.

I did not, of course, ignore Alex's behavior. When I felt that Alex behaved in a bossy or aggressive way toward me, I pointed it out or asked questions that suggested how certain words can lead to unintended reactions by others. Thus, I did work on the specific behaviors that others did not like about Alex, but in a way that was more long-term and, perhaps unfortunately but unavoidably, slower.

Ultimately, Taylor and Alex figured out their working relationship. How did this happen? By design, I'm not certain because I deliberately was not directly involved; I just coached each person separately, and this coaching naturally decreased over time. While Taylor and Alex never became close friends, they worked together for almost a decade in the same group, long after I had moved on to another part of the organization. I am certain they must have had their disagreements over the years, but I hope that my coaching contributed to their continued work.

This result illustrates that sometimes an interpersonal problem cannot be fixed. The aggrieved person might need to live with a less-than-perfect, annoying situation. Coach the person to develop a mindset so that the situation's sharpness becomes duller, even if the problems do not entirely disappear.

RULE 3: When talking about management problems, focus on behaviors, not feelings. Behaviors are directly observable; feelings are inferred. Seek out what the aggrieved person wants to see, concretely.

This rule derives directly from a management book I read— *The One Minute Manager.* It's the only one I (consciously) got from a book and applied to work situations.

I found this rule useful for shifting the conversation with employees into more practical, actionable directions. Often employees would talk to me about something in the workplace that was bothering them—their stress, another employee, or frustration with the workplace. This conversation would always begin with the employee telling me that they felt unappreciated, disrespected, angry, or stressed—"Emilia doesn't respect my expertise." However, it's difficult to directly fix the employee's feelings (or beliefs) about another person's attitudes or thoughts about the aggrieved employee.

In these cases, I would try to shift the conversation to concrete, observable behaviors: "If individuals are not respecting your expertise, what does that look like? Do they not acknowledge your contributions at meetings? Do they interrupt you? Do they not invite you to meetings?" Once we know the behaviors that the employee doesn't like, we can begin to work on solutions. I would ask, "What do you want to see happen?" Often, at first, the employee would switch back to thoughts and feelings: "I want Emilia to think about me as an expert." I again would shift the conversation to behaviors: "What would that look like? How should Emilia behave if she is treating you as an expert?" If the employee caught on to the idea of concrete behaviors, we could develop a plan for addressing concerns. For example, the employee could talk with Emilia about being invited to meetings or could have strategies for dealing with interruptions (and maybe get some additional training on this skill).

Ken was a junior researcher, put in charge of a team that was implementing one of his ideas in software. He was having trouble with one of the visual designers, Harrison, who had many years of experience working on these types of projects.

At an update meeting, Ken was clearly upset and said, "Irv, I'm getting tired of Harrison. He doesn't respect my leadership."

I responded, "What does Harrison do when you feel like he isn't respecting your leadership?"

"He just doesn't act like I'm the project leader. He thinks that he's in charge and we all have to listen to him."

"What's an example of that? Give me something concrete that you've actually seen."

"Well, he interrupts me and others a lot . . . he tears down other people's ideas and won't budge if someone doesn't like his idea."

This began to sound familiar; I had worked with Harrison and others in his area.

"This has happened to me as well, with Harrison and others from that group. The visual design group can seem adversarial. The issue is that they have high standards, so people in that group constantly criticize others' work and defend their own. Ultimately, they compromise, but argument is part of their work process.

"Does Harrison contribute to the project? He is coming up with designs?"

"Oh, yes, sure. But no matter what I do, he won't change anything. The product is supposed to come from my research in this area, but if Harrison goes off on his own, we can't use anything he gives us."

"I've worked with Harrison, so know what you mean. But Harrison's a good designer. He likes a challenge, but he's assertive when defending his work and criticizing others' work. Try this: when

Harrison wants to go in one direction, ask him to also produce something that's closer to your vision."

This approach seemed to work, with the project continuing and Ken feeling better about working with Harrison. With multiple designs coming from Harrison, he was more amenable to adjustments.

But the real breakthrough was in Ken's interpretation of Harrison's behavior. He stopped seeing Harrison's disagreement as, perhaps, a challenge for control of the group. Ken started to reinterpret Harrison's behavior as a reflection of his expertise and his high standards. Harrison might still interrupt and could still be disagreeable, but Ken began to learn how to work with those behaviors.

This rule of focusing on behaviors is similar to what you read in Rule 1 about not jumping to conclusions. Except that here, instead of you, the manager, jumping to conclusions, it is your employee who is doing the jumping. In both cases, collecting more information is key. For the current rule, you are guiding the employee to gather more information, or giving them more information, to help the employee reinterpret events and see what actions could lead to a successful resolution.

Also reflected here is Rule 2 about not getting directly involved in employee relationships. As a manager, it would have been a mistake for me to have spoken directly with Harrison or served as a facilitator at one of the meetings. Instead, I mentored one of the people in a conflict about how to look at someone else's behavior in a new light by focusing on concrete behaviors.

RULE 4: Make sure you have all the information before you escalate a challenge to upper management.

Even as a manager, your interactions with upper management are likely to be limited. You need to be strategic in those interactions and not bring minor, day-to-day issues that you, as a manager, should be able to handle. There will certainly be cases where you ask for advice—after all, your upper-level managers likely have more experience than you do at being a manager, so can act as your mentors. But if you are requesting more resources or alerting them of a problem, be strategic.

Upper-level managers, have a broader view of the organization than individual contributors or their immediate managers. They naturally think in terms of groups of people and how those groups fit together to pursue some area strategy. Upper-level managers are accountable to their own managers and have different performance objectives and metrics. For example, whereas a portion of a scientist's performance might be measured by the number and quality of publications and presentations they produce in a year (with those disseminations all working toward the scientist's general research strategy), the metrics of the immediate manager of a group of scientists might go beyond numbers to include items such as

- the breadth of research dissemination (research appears in a variety of journals or conferences),
- the degree of collaboration within their group and across groups, and
- the extent to which the totality of the group's disseminations supports the research strategy or mission of the group.

The metrics for upper-level managers would be at a broader level still, such as related to working towards an organization-wide research agenda, staffing levels in strategic areas of expertise, or partnerships with other organizations.

Communications with upper-level management should be conducted in a way that is consistent with that manager's needs when everything is going well. When everything is *not* going well and there's an issue that must be brought to their attention, you must understand how the manager will perceive this issue and how best to present it to achieve your goal—whether that goal is, for example, to involve HR in an employee dispute, to get more resources (an admittedly broad category that includes funds, extra time from existing employees, or hiring of new employees), or to have an employee transferred from one group to another.

To frame an issue correctly for escalation, it is absolutely, 100% critical to have a lot (I hesitate to say "all," but that's what I'd like to say) of information about the issue. This point might seem obvious, but it is surprisingly difficult to achieve. Many times, I have brought an issue to my manager based almost solely on an employee's judgment that an issue exists. Inevitably, I later discover details about the issue that suggests the escalation was not necessary or that I framed the issue incorrectly. More embarrassingly, in some cases, the manager to whom I was escalating started to ask for some basic context about the issue, and I was unable to provide detailed answers.

Whereas it might not be possible to find out the full context of an issue, you should at least ask some basic questions. Start with Who, What, Where, Why, and How, if nothing else. Try to get a concrete "ask" from the person raising the issue—what would that person like to see happen? Probe the rationale for the request. You might not get all the information, but at least you will have more context for your request to upper-level management. Take the point of view that your ability to escalate (and get results) from upper-level management is a finite resource and that each request has a cost. Make sure you want to spend your capital on this request and, if so, that you are clear as to the rationale for the request.

An example of this rule in action occurred when the director of a group in my area made requests. This group was responsible for helping other areas in the organization integrate new technology into their products and conducting tests of how well that integration worked. Unfortunately, this group was chronically understaffed, and the amount of work to be done was always more than its members could easily handle, even with the growing number of professionals in that group.

At the same time, the director and other staff in that group were extremely resourceful and flexible—they were able to come up with solutions and handle many of the requests that came in. However, the director tended to escalate issues to me. For example, one time the group was short-staffed for a particular user testing session. The director told me that they needed a few extra research assistants to help with that testing. I took him at his word and immediately escalated the issue, making the request to my manager and some managers in other areas. I received approval to move some people from other groups to supply this need. However, by the end of that very same day, the day of the initial request, after I had spent the day obtaining additional staff for him, the group director told me that they had figured out a better scheduling approach, and so no longer needed the help. I had expended some of my escalation capital for no reason.

What I learned from this (and similar incidents) was to ask more questions before escalating an issue: When was the additional resource needed by? What would be involved in training other people to help, and was that feasible? I also learned to wait—if the request was not an immediate need (the director planned enough ahead such that it rarely was), I did nothing for at least twenty-four hours. In most cases, the director or his staff would have figured out a solution to their current crisis by then.

Questions About Crises

1. Think of a recent crisis where you had to make a decision. What type of additional information about the crisis did you gather (or should you have gathered) before acting? How did you test your understanding of the situation before dealing with the crisis?

2. Are there situations in which you often find yourself responding before gathering more information? List out several situations, then reflect on that list. What defines these situations, and how might you remind yourself to gather more information first rather than responding hastily?

3. Reflect on an escalated crisis where the initial steps taken were based on insufficient information. What would have been a more effective approach, and how could this have altered the outcome?

4. Consider a time when your involvement in a co-worker dispute might have prevented a more effective resolution. What would have been an alternative approach, and how could coaching have empowered the individuals involved?

Alternatively, consider a time when you chose to coach rather than directly intervene. How did the parties involved respond?

SECTION II: PERSUASION

Persuasion is how you get things done as a manager. Persuasion is often seen as the primary way to get resources for your group; you persuade upper management that it is in the best interest of the organization to take a particular course of action or make a particular decision. Similarly, one must persuade peer managers to collaborate or compromise to allocate limited resources.

Less is said about persuading people who report to you. Sure, you could order them to do something, but isn't it healthier for the organization for employees to be happy? To be taking a course of action because they agree it's in their best interest? To feel that they are contributing to the health of the organization? To deal with setbacks or corporate changes flexibly and without a loss of morale?

RULE 5: Sometimes people need to make their own decisions. You can nudge them in the direction you want, but they need to reach conclusions by themselves. Other people don't mind as much if, occasionally, a decision is made for them. Still other people must have the feeling that each decision they make is their own. Let them.

Managing scientists is like herding cats—you exert a small influence on their direction. That small influence may have an overall cumulative effect, but the cat is going to go wherever it wants to go. Even a junior scientist will have several years of experience building (sometimes world-class) expertise in a particular area. The most junior individuals likely have a level of expertise and experience seen in more senior-level people in some other areas. By the time they first join the organization, even fresh out of graduate school, they will have given several presentations at professional conferences, authored a few professional publications (i.e., they are published authors), contributed to the writing of a few government grants, or sometimes directed or at least mentored others in the conducting of research.

Managing scientists (and, often, many employees) has more to do with nudging, suggesting, requesting, and asking questions than with making assignments. This was my approach whereas my peer managers sometimes were much more directive. In my experience, very directive managers were common.

A senior scientist in my group wanted to be a manager. She had a traditional view of management—as a means to career advancement. Once you achieve a certain level of prominence as a scientist, you become a manager of scientists. However, unlike at some institutions, managing scientists does not mean that they work for you. They are not going to be directly assigned to help you with your research or to do research that you are then automatically a co-author on. I'm not sure, but I think that's the expectation that she might have had.

At the time, I did not think she was suited to management. I had worked with several scientists who became successful managers, and she struck me as someone who would be happier and more successful gaining more and more prominence as an even more senior scientist—whether through promotion (although the scientist line only had one or two more levels), by wielding greater influence on the organization (e.g., presenting her work to the Board of Trustees, influencing some type of corporate policy or a business process based on her research), or more success in obtaining external grants (which "buys" autonomy). She was (and still is) a brilliant scientist, focused on an area that contributes much to science and has direct applications to the practices of measurement and education. Why in the world would she want to be distracted by management?

However, while both her direct manager and I stated our judgments, she was not to be "herded." She saw management as the next logical step in her career. At the next opportunity, I made her a manager and had three other scientists report to her—another manager had left the group, providing this opportunity.

For several months, she met with these scientists, mentored them, and provided feedback on their plans, analyses, and papers She attended meetings that I held semi-monthly with the managers in my area to discuss both personnel issues and issues related to the overall strategy and work for the center. She approved timesheets, gave feedback on promotion cases, and helped out when personnel issues arose. Of course, she received mentoring and guidance from her former manager and me to help her make her way as a new manager.

It quickly became apparent to this person that management was a daunting amount work, much of which did not further her research. Plus, although she collaborated with one of her direct reports, her work with the others involved learning about *their* research and what *they* needed. After a few months, this person asked to be moved back to a senior scientist position. At the next opportunity, I was able to do that, providing someone else, perhaps more suited to the work, an opportunity to try.

Being a manager means putting your work on hold to a certain extent. It means putting others' needs ahead of your own. A good manager's contribution to science is to nudge people toward particular areas of research that would be beneficial to the field and the organization. The senior scientist had to come to this understanding on her own.

Of course, I could have simply told the person that her chief contribution to the organization was as an individual contributor, rather than as a manager. I could have offered to put her in line for a promotion to a higher scientist level and simply not entertained the notion of her becoming a manager. But what do you think might have happened? Lower morale? Her transferring to another group or organization that would fulfill her desire for management? By being able to make her own decision, she both appreciated her current role, remained committed to our group, and gained valuable experience that might serve her later if she chooses to pursue management again.

RULE 6: Pave the way. Persuasion takes time and can be an extended process. People are more receptive to ideas that they have heard before, so informal discussion of ideas early can eventually lead to persuasion later.

People like what they've heard or seen before. Some people have a bias for the first information they receive on a topic, weighing all positive and negative evidence about a topic in comparison with that first bit of information. If a VP's first experience with—or the first thing they hear about—a new employee involves the person complaining, there is a danger that the VP will always expect (and therefore more highly remember and believe) to hear about that employee complaining in the future. This also goes along with the saying that "you don't get a second chance to make a first impression," implying the importance of that first impression. Many research studies suggest this type of primacy effect—first items are remembered better, and new information is colored by what's heard first (confirmation bias).

It can be very difficult to change these first impressions, but it can be done with deliberation, planning, and effort.

A director had a negative encounter with a senior scientist. They had worked together on a proposal, and the director thought that the senior scientist didn't produce a draft that was as persuasive as the director could have done, even if the general content was fine. This interaction colored the director's perceptions of the senior scientist, who had already had a long, successful career of conducting well-regarded research and creating innovative products and procedures. There were several possible reasons why the initial collaboration between the director and scientist didn't go well, but the important point was that it was the first extended interaction between them. That interaction colored both of their perceptions of each other for the next year or more.

Eventually, I became the director of that senior scientist, and the director became the senior director above me. I knew that this scientist had proven to be valuable to the organization, yet I saw the senior director subtlety sidelining him from work. He noticed this and had started talking about leaving the organization. From that point forward, I made an effort to point out the scientist's successes—without going overboard—if his name or work came up during a meeting. I particularly focused on the scientist's concrete contributions to real-world applications, his mentoring of other scientists, and his leadership and value. Slowly over time, the senior director's appraisal of him seemed to change. This persuasion took more than a year.

The important point of this story is *not* about my powers of persuasion or how to manipulate someone into changing their mind. The important point is that a first impression can take a *long* time to overcome. And, like it or not, those first impressions can have an impact on an employee's morale, on business decisions regarding the employee, and even on the employee's decision to seek employment elsewhere. I'm not faulting the director—the cognitive impact of a first impression is well-documented and overwhelming. Given everything else the director had to deal with, that level of effort for one person (of many talented senior scientists) would be difficult.

Pave the way. Something that goes along with first impressions, in terms of persuasion, is the cumulative effect of repeated exposure to an idea. If you are going to make a request or want to advocate for a decision, it takes more than one interaction to make a case. Very, very few times have I made a case for, say, more resources for my group and had it approved immediately. Successful arguing or persuasion takes a long time, even if you are not battling against a bad first impression.

Paving the way is sometimes called socializing an idea. The concept is that you bring up the idea informally, getting people's impressions of it and their feedback. Get the counterarguments that reflect people's knee-jerk reactions. Bring up the idea again, informally, at a later time, perhaps addressing some of the counterarguments (e.g., acknowledging them but also providing concrete reasons why they might not apply). For example, let's say I know an employee will be coming up for promotion. I would *not* just make the case to my supervisor and inundate him with information, trying to formulate the perfect argument. Instead, I would first mention that the person under consideration seems to have been doing well for a while and seems due for a promotion. At another meeting, maybe once the employee had begun to write up his or her promotion case, I would mention the promotion again, bringing up particularly strong evidence from the person's case. I would listen to any concerns that the supervisor had, and provide counterexamples either then or later. Thus, it might be that I start talking about the promotion two to three months before formally bringing it to my supervisor's promotion review group.

Just as I would socialize an idea with a supervisor, I would take a similar approach with my direct reports. If I know that an organizational change might occur (but am not allowed to talk about it) or that a change will soon be happening in the type of research that will be prioritized next year, I would find ways to communicate that to the relevant employees. Not to reveal any information that I was not allowed to, but to pave the way. To give the employees an indication that a change is happening so that when the change occurs, they will not be overwhelmed or surprised.

In the case of new research priorities, this topic might come up when I'm talking with scientists about their current research or plans for next year. I would show more interest in the work that's closer to the type of work that would likely be emphasized. Again, this was not manipulation but rather trying to subtly shift people's emphasis or at least give them insight into what higher-level management was planning.

RULE 7: Sometimes feedback must be delayed. Give it when the other person is ready to hear it, not just when it occurs to you.

Few people like to hear criticism. Our first reaction, almost instinctual, is to be defensive. We want to argue why the criticism is invalid, reflects a misunderstanding of a situation, or was someone else's fault. Whether or not these points are valid, when we try to explain away a criticism, we really aren't listening. We aren't trying to understand the points and aren't ready to reflect on how we might change our behavior in the future. Instead, we're focusing on why the feedback isn't correct, the circumstances that likely led to the feedback, and trying to attribute the feedback to something other than our own behavior.

This dismissing of feedback when we aren't prepared to hear it is natural. We tend to view ourselves positively, and information that contradicts this might be dismissed in some ways.

Of course, we might also have another type of knee-jerk reaction, that the feedback reflects that we are not as talented at something as we thought we were. Again, even if we accept the feedback, the criticism might feel personal, so again, we are not really listening but over-attributing weight to it. Instead of dismissing it, we are letting it crush us.

I have seen both of these extreme reactions, and others, in people to whom I've given feedback. The common theme is that the person is not listening to the feedback and reflecting on it but rather focusing their energies on dismissing or overly interpreting it.

When might a person not take feedback in the manner it was intended? If the feedback is a surprise, the person might get defensive. Similarly, if the feedback is delivered when the person is stressed or otherwise very busy, the feedback is unlikely to have the desired effect.

The problem is that we managers might think of the feedback in the moment and want to deliver it then. The reasoning seems to be: When better to correct a mistake than immediately when it happens? That way, the feedback occurs at a time when the person has just made an error. However, I don't agree with this point of view. Feedback needs to be given when it will do the most good. Plus, feedback must be given when the person is ready to hear it, understand it, and reflect on it.

The effective delivery of feedback relates to two of the themes you might have noticed in this book. One theme is that so much in management is not a single event, but an accumulation of small events. In the current case, feedback isn't just given once. It can be given in small doses over time. Feedback reflects a desire for someone to change their behavior. That doesn't typically happen in just one shot; over time, the person learns new behaviors that incorporate feedback.

The second theme related to feedback is that managers work in service of the people who report to them. Feedback is for the employees' benefit, not for the manager's. Thus, managers have to be certain their employees are ready to hear the feedback. Many management books focus on strategies to give feedback, such as the "criticism sandwich," where positive feedback is encased in some negative feedback. But little is said about giving feedback over a longer period, on multiple occasions, to allow the person time to internalize the feedback and to learn from it.

A manager, Robin, who reported to me, had the habit of writing very long emails to justify a decision or recommend a course of action. These emails were well argued, with able justification. The more important the recommendation, or the more urgent the matter, the longer the emails would become. Similarly, when we were asked to give weekly updates to higher management, the updates about Robin's own work as well as the work of the people they managed would be overly long, containing an abundance of detail.

Upper management would rarely read these extended emails. My supervisor would ask me for a summary of the email, adding to my workload (admittedly nowadays I'd have AI write a summary and then edit it). Before passing along the group's updates, I would need to pull out the key elements that were of particular interest to my managers. I would share these summaries with Robin, asking for shorter initial emails or justifications. However, this had no effect. Robin would respond with detailed explanations that could only be described as excruciating. They wanted to present the group's work in the best light and believed that the way to do this was to describe every little detail of the group members' work.

This continued for some time until Robin was recommending someone for promotion. To justify a promotion, we had to complete a table with evidence of how the person already met the requirements in the job description for each aspect of the new position. Working with the person to be promoted,

Robin produced a table that was three times as long as any other promotion justification I had seen. This time, rather than reducing the table for Robin and the employee, I passed it along in its current length to my supervisor, who was the decision maker on the promotion. He gave the feedback that I had been giving: the justifications were too long.

I discussed this feedback with Robin in light of the similar feedback I had given previously. As we did before, we discussed how these sorts of overly long justifications could distract from her main points. We talked about how if higher-level managers were given extra information, they would have to decide which aspects were the most important and might not make the same selections Robin would.

This time, Robin listened. This attentiveness likely stemmed from wanting to do well by the person being promoted and not wanting to hurt that person's chances. As a result, Robin was ready to listen to and internalize the feedback. A shorter justification table was submitted, and the person received her promotion.

I would like to end this story by saying that Robin then produced emails and updates that were always short and to the point. Unfortunately, when stressed or in a time crunch, Robin's writing remained just as lengthy as before. However, when given time to reflect, Robin started to produce much more pointed and focused emails.

RULE 8: Ambiguity begets anxiety. What might seem like giving people choices or agency instead results in feelings of anxiousness. Strive to be definitive when possible; when not possible, try to limit the ambiguity.

You might feel like you are giving people choices or agency when you leave a situation open-ended, but often an ambiguous situation just makes people more anxious. Having choice is not always a good thing. In UX (user experience) design, we learn that choice can actually *decrease* the speed with which people use an interface. When people are given multiple paths to get something done, they have to decide which path to take. That decision-making slows people down and makes the interface harder to use than one that doesn't accommodate so many different paths.

This type of ambiguity shows up often in manager-employee interactions. Let's say you are providing advice on a research paper a junior employee is planning to write. You are familiar with the research, having worked on the project, and know that there are different ways of presenting the work. You might discuss the alternative organizations of the paper and then ask the employee to make a decision, write up a first draft, and send it to you for feedback. However, I've found that such an approach can slow down the writing process and ramp up anxiety. The junior scientist (of course, it depends on the scientist) might spend a lot of time deciding which paper outline is best and have trouble getting started (i.e., actually writing). Simply having choices can impede progress.

Instead, a mentoring session might begin with a discussion of the different possible paper outlines but end with a specific choice. Based on the discussion, the manager and employee together select one outline to pursue. Even if the employee ultimately decides on another outline (after all, the employee does have agency), perhaps when writing the first draft, starting out with a single next step reduces anxiety and, I've found, leads to better results.

Another example of ambiguity came in the form of a new internal research proposal process. People were told that larger projects with multiple subprojects (i.e., larger, multi-functional teams) would be preferred over the previous process of individual projects (i.e., projects with just one or two scientists and other staff). People were told they could self-organize into larger projects or propose smaller projects that might be later organized by higher management into larger projects. Among other benefits, the new process was intended to make proposal writing less burdensome and quicker. Rather than each person writing two to three proposals, a scientist might only need to contribute a few paragraphs to two to three larger proposals, for example.

Nevertheless, the ambiguity in the new process increased anxiety. Considerable time was spent strategizing a good approach: propose your own project that forwards your research goals in a way consistent with the published yearly research priorities (i.e., convincing the reader that your project is consistent with those priorities), or embed your work within a larger project that's pursuing a priority more directly, alleviating the need to argue for your own project, but potentially risking loss of agency (one project within a larger group). This strategizing caused much anxiety and re-writing of proposals, making the process difficult and leading to lower morale for a time.

With the benefit of hindsight, taking away some of the ambiguity in the new process might have led to less anxiety. A more straightforward approach might have been either to (a) say that only larger projects were to be proposed and that everyone had to collaborate and figure out the structure of those larger projects or (b) declare that everyone should propose smaller projects and the research leaders would decide how to combine them into larger projects. That is, be clear about the type of proposal that is acceptable. At the same time, the first option might have been better as the second option would create anxiety because people didn't know how their projects would be combined with others (although the anxiety in that case would come from the unknown rather than too many choices).

Of course, the anxiety stemmed not just from ambiguity but also from the newness of the proposal process. As you will see in the next rule (Rule 9), people can react negatively to change and cannot be expected to see the benefits of the change immediately. *Any* change causes anxiety, and when a new process is introduced, sufficient time for people to process the change in their own minds is needed.

As a manager, part of my job was to sell the new process to the scientists—to persuade them of the benefits to their work. To do this, I pointed out the similarities with other proposal writing approaches that had been used in the past and helped guide proposal writers through the ambiguities in the process. For instance, larger projects were often created when writing proposals for research grants to government agencies. These were procedures and approaches the scientists were familiar with, so by pointing out the similarity, I hoped to reduce the sense that the new internal process was a change. I also tried to reduce ambiguity by insisting that people write proposals for larger projects, effectively eliminating the choice of the smaller proposal. Obviously, if a scientist was very insistent on writing a smaller proposal, that was fine because that person had already made their choice. However, *removing* choice for others created less anxiety about having to select the proposal writing strategy.

Finally, I worked to keep people calm generally and encouraged the managers in the center to do likewise. It would serve no purpose to say things like "Yeah, this new process sucks, but what can you do?" I did point out some of the difficulties but also tried to help people to address the challenges. Sometimes I was there just to hear someone vent, without providing any advice. Overall, there was still much anxiety among some groups of scientists, but in the end, everyone created their proposals.

RULE 9: People need time to process either good or bad news, or even neutral news that represents a change. Give them a heads up, then the official news.

Why is a rule like this in a section on persuasion? I learned that as a manager, part of your job is to keep the work environment calm. You want people to focus on their work and the activities that facilitate their work. Ideally, they should not be worrying about how changes to the organization as a whole, to the research priorities of the R&D division, or to upper management will impact their day-to-day work. In other words, change more often related to people's working environment rather than to their work *per se*. These changes do not tend to affect day-to-day work in any meaningful way. Thus, when some type of change occurred, or was about to occur, I found it best to persuade people not to overreact and to just focus on their work.

Change makes anyone uncomfortable. There is a tendency for people to focus on the change, such as to be anxious about how the change might affect them or what it means for their employment (even during times of high morale). After all, when we hear about a change—whether a change in management structure, someone joining our group, some new procedure—we do not truly know how that change will affect us, and "ambiguity begets anxiety."

As a manager, you need to allow people time to process what the change means. You cannot just announce a change without warning and expect people to appreciate what is good about it (or why it will not affect them). With time, and a little persuasion, the employees in your group might see that the change has negligible effect on their day-to-day work.

For example, most of the time, the scientists that reported to me just wanted to do their research. They wanted to focus on collecting or analyzing data, writing up research, writing proposals for research, talking with others about their research, or designing experiments to collect data. These are the core elements of why they became scientists. Similarly, the software engineers wanted to design and create software or show off what they created to peers or to those who had requested the software. In other words, people want to focus on their work.

Thus, it is not surprising that the people in my group, and employees generally, do not react well to change. Change might mean they will need to work on something new or work on something in a new way. Something as simple as a change to the name of the research center we were in, even if we came up with the new name, could be a source of anxiety: "Will I be able to continue my project if the topic doesn't quite fit with the new name for the center?"

Here is an example that occurred several times: Let's say there was a *chance* that a new employee would be joining our center. Where would be the best fit for this person? I would think about which of my managers would work best with this person (see the rules on organizational structure), then have a discussion with that manager. I would hedge the discussion (after all, the transfer might not occur), but I would at least let the manager know that there is a possibility. Depending on the situation, I might not even be allowed to discuss the name of the transferred employee. Nevertheless, by bringing the possibility to the manager's attention, if the new assignment does come to pass, I have allowed them the time to accommodate to the new situation.

Sometimes changes can be seen from further away; they might not happen, and if they do, it might be several months in the future. Nevertheless, I have found it useful to gently hint at possible changes. Even a little bit of "heads up" helps people process news and make it feel not so sudden. It provides people with a sense of control in that they have time to think about the news and figure out how they will accommodate it into their working life.

Questions About Persuasion

1. Think of a work situation in which you must persuade someone on a decision. How can you pave the way toward this decision over time? How can you break down the material to use in making the decision and deliver it during different, say, update sessions with your manager or with someone who reports to you?

2. Consider a scenario where your attempt to give a team member a decision-making role led to anxiety rather than empowerment. What might have caused this reaction, and how could you manage such situations differently in the future? Recall a situation where being definitive in your communication helped to alleviate anxiety or confusion. How can you apply this lesson to the earlier situation?

3. When persuading someone to embrace a significant change, how do you assess that person's readiness to receive and process the information? What preparation steps might you take?

4. Think about a moment when you delayed giving feedback, waiting for the right time. How did you determine that the time was right, and how was the feedback received? Alternatively, think about some feedback that you currently need to give to someone. How might you pave the way to prepare the person to receive the feedback?

SECTION III: TRUST

Management is easier when there is mutual trust. The people in your group trust that you work with their best interests, and the best interests of the organization, in mind. They trust that even if you make a decision that they are not happy with, at least you are working from a trustworthy place. They trust your judgment—not because you are their boss, but because they have seen your judgment in action. They trust that you are not working (solely) from your self-interest. Management is also easier when your peer managers (and upper management) trust you. Again, even if they know you might put your group ahead of their group, they still know that you are fundamentally a good person and want what's best for the organization. That you would not be treating them disrespectfully—that you will never backstab them.

Without all the politics and infighting that come with mistrust (or lack of trust), one can focus on management issues such as morale, personnel interactions, resource needs, and productivity.

Building trust takes time, as the rules in this section imply, but the payoff is considerable.

RULE 10: Have informal get-togethers with fellow managers. These meet-ups build trust, making any official, work-based interactions (e.g., other meetings or requests in either direction) easier.

Your fellow managers are your peers but also your competitors. After all, there are limited resources within a company—e.g., job slots, money for research or travel, office space, and admin support. If one manager's group gets a resource, it means another manager does not get that resource. With enough resources, this limitation doesn't matter, i.e., if everyone is getting sufficient resources to get their group's work done and keep people engaged, fulfilled, and productive. But how often does that happen?

This competition need not be completely zero-sum, however. If managers have a sense of shared goals, of all doing what's necessary for the good of the organization (or of a larger community) as a whole, then trade-offs, turn-taking, give-and-take, or mutual concessions help distribute the limited resources in ways that, over time, lift all boats. The basis for the necessary negotiations is trust.

Building trust takes time. I'm sure there are many theories about how two people establish trust, but I doubt if it can happen solely within the confines of regular work as peer managers. The day-to-day of being a manager has you constantly thinking about resources (either directly or indirectly) and what might make your job easier. Area meetings with fellow managers (e.g., your common supervisor) do not seem like the proper places to build mutual trust—they seem instead to be where competition is fiercest.

Instead, I found that the best place to build trust is informal meetings—over lunch or coffee. Just a regular time to get together, without an agenda. Sometimes we would chat about our families, home improvement projects, issues with neighbors, hobbies, or experiences from our lives. Occasionally, we would talk about our respective groups. This topic is natural. After all, your fellow managers are the only ones who can fully appreciate what your day-to-day work is like. They are having the same struggles (how to get their non-management work done while supporting everyone in their group; how to deal with unexpected requests from a client or the boss) as you are. Again, there wasn't a purpose or goal to the get-together beyond the get-togethers themselves. These informal gatherings built trust. They communicated that I was a good person, with the best interests of others at heart, and my fellow managers were similarly motivated. Or, if not so altruist, at least we knew more about who each other was as a person. And that's enough.

With this trust, when we had to compete, and even at the update meetings, negotiations went smoother. We could challenge each other a little without the situation getting too acrimonious. We were more willing to give in and be (temporarily) on the losing side of a concession, knowing that we'd be on the winning side in the future. Of course, things didn't work out perfectly—some managers were more aggressive and tended to get more resources for their groups.

That's the theory, at least. In practice, it depends on the people, of course. For example, one fellow manager and I met at a coffee shop, once a month, before work. This seemed like the most successful of my meetings—we made the most progress in trust over time. Being off-site and meeting before the workday likely helped because we didn't have a good excuse for skipping the meeting. I then reached out to two other managers, and we met for lunch. Those were more likely to be canceled. One of the managers was already a friend—we had been to each other's houses and knew each other's families. Thus, the level of trust was already quite high, and these meetings didn't change much. Still, it was nice to get together and vent. The third manager, who canceled most often, had a slow building of trust. The degree of competition ("my group's work is the most important for the organization") started quite high and lessened just a bit. Occasionally, he would allow my group to get some resources when we were in direct competition. Not often, however. I don't know whether more regular meetings or meetings off-site would have made a difference.

The lesson here is that there is no one strategy that will work with all of your peer managers. You will find that informal get-togethers work well, but when and how you arrange them will depend on the individuals involved. As a manager, building trust with your colleagues is a long-term goal; it takes time, and may require adjustments, but greatly eases your life as a manager.

RULE 11: *Every once in a while, drop by someone's office, especially if you don't see them often. The conversations could be about work or just life, but it's important to maintain connections.*

This rule is equivalent to the previous one but focuses on people in your group (and elsewhere, but that's networking and this book is about management). As more people report to you (directly or indirectly), it's common to have more contact with some people vs. others. However, everyone should feel a part of your group; you shouldn't be delegating that sense of belonging to the direct manager of employees. Doing so might lead to silos within your group where employees feel that they are a part of each manager's group rather than a part of your overall group or center.

At least once a week, I would drop by someone's office to whom I hadn't spoken in a while. As the rule says, the conversations would just be catching up on work or life, not a formal update. Instead, I preferred a spontaneous how's-it-going to a scheduled meeting to avoid the feeling that the employee had to prepare or felt that they were being evaluated. "How did last week's data collection go?" "What do you think of your new apartment?" "Has your son been enjoying his new school?" "How are the beehives doing?"—these are the range of questions I would ask (tailored to the individual, of course).

It's especially important to drop by people who are working remotely. When some people are on-site and others are remote, it creates an unfortunate dichotomy, and remote workers can feel cut off. Not everyone, but it's something to watch. When everyone was remote during the 2020 global pandemic, this wasn't an issue—we were all in the same boat and every interaction was occurring online. However, during my time as a manager, I typically had three to six people out of thirty who were remote, and I made sure to drop in on them occasionally and also to have face-to-face meetings whenever they were on site.

Over the course of a few months, I would systematically visit with the many people in my center. If they were on-site, I would drop by their offices and chat for a couple of minutes. If they worked remotely, I would send a message asking for a quick video chat. (I would be careful to word it like "nothing serious; I just wanted to catch up.") Sometimes I would take notes so that I could follow up the next time, but often I remembered some details of the previous conversation, which might have been a couple months earlier, to follow up. Occasionally I might find out about some out-of-work achievement—finishing a particularly challenging knitted sweater, hearing from a school applied to, a child graduating, and so forth. With their permission, I acknowledged those types of achievements at center meetings or through small hallway celebrations. At these celebrations, I would also go out of my way to talk with people I typically didn't have the opportunity to chat with individually.

Of course, I also shared some of my own personal details in these informal chats, helping the employee to see me as a person and not only the boss. However, I would be careful not to over share—I once had a manager who, over time, provided quite a bit of detailed information about his psychological motivations due to his upbringing—but most people knew a little bit about my children, hobbies, and schooling. When you are talking with someone in your group, remember that you are still the leader. Thus, you are fair game for others to talk about behind your back. It's not something I worried about often, but I only shared personal stories with one employee if I felt comfortable that all the employees in my group would eventually know about it.

Why build trust in this way? Trust is critical when decisions come from "on high," without warning, and it is up to you as a manager to deliver the news—whether bad news, neutral news which represents a change, or good news. Maintaining connections with everyone in your group—personal, one-on-one connections—even if only occasionally, helps build this level of trust.

RULE 12: *You must get your hands dirty. You cannot effectively advise a project unless you sit through real project meetings: working meetings or updates where the project details get discussed. Much won't seem immediately relevant, but that detritus undergirds later high-level decisions about that project.*

As a manager of scientists, people want your advice. Unfortunately, it is difficult to give that advice if you know only a little bit about their project. That's inevitable when you have a large group. However, if you are going to give project-related advice regularly, you have to be directly engaged in the project.

I have seen people try to advise projects on an ongoing basis by only occasionally attending update meetings and never attending working meetings. Of course, there are some high-level points of feedback you can provide. However, to be an advisor, consultant, or mentor to a project, you have to get your hands dirty with the details of the project and the rationale behind various project decisions. You have to have been part of the project's decision-making, such as deciding on taking one approach to data collection or data analysis rather than another.

You also have to truly be part of the team, meaning that you accept or volunteer for work assignments just as any other team member would, attend many project meetings, and remain responsible for any deliverables or other work that's owed to other team members. In other words, even as a senior scientist or a manager, you become one of the gang.

Acting in this way on the project, accepting the leadership of the principal investigator (even if that person reports to you), builds trust. The project members know that they can count on you, and they see what you are capable of—not just as a manager, but as a teammate. It also makes the task of being a manager more palatable because you get to participate deeply in research, which I always found difficult to do as a manager. I never felt I had the bandwidth to be both a manager and a researcher, at least once I became a senior manager and the number of people in my group went from about ten to about thirty-five. Being a manager of scientists, as I've noted throughout this book, involves a set of skills and activities that are related to research, and that are informed by having been a researcher, but it's distinct from being a researcher. I could be a good manager, or I could lead projects, but I could not do both. I know that some managers manage to have their pet projects, and I did manage to write book chapters or journal papers (based on previous research I had done), but I never again was a project leader, a loss I knew might happen and that fed into my initial reluctance to be a manager.

However, I was a team member on a couple of research and development projects—attending project meetings, taking on assignments, and contributing to the writing up of results. (Admittedly, I wasn't always a great teammate, as I typically had such small amounts of time.) These activities helped to build trust; I heard more about project difficulties (even on other projects from my teammates) rather than only receiving the rosy reports that you sometimes get as a manager.

Obviously, you cannot be a full-time member of all projects in your group. You have to be selective, although those selections should change from year to year (or whatever timeframe works best at your organization). Try to select projects where your presence would do the most good to the project or in building trust within your group. For example, one project I joined was led by a junior researcher and included some other junior researchers who were recently hired. None reported directly to me, and so by being on the project they got to know me as a researcher (rather than a manager) and I got to know them.

RULE 13: *Every so often, thank people. A sincere form of thanks is when you can say how this person has helped you personally. That is, not as a manager thanking an employee for "a job well-done," but as a colleague thanking another colleague: "You have made a difference in my work."*

I admit to not being great at concretely and directly thanking people. I'm always polite and probably say "thanks" for lots of little things, but the sincere feedback of "thank you" doesn't come naturally to me. Even though I am sincere, sometimes to my ears I sound fake. Thus, I've spent some time thinking about how to communicate my appreciation of someone, along with gestures, body language, and the right words. I don't want to be taken as insincere when I mean to express appreciation. I try to look the person in the eye, speak slowly, and say something like, "Wow—this is really fantastic work. It is going to help people do X, Y, Z." Or "I appreciate that being a manager hasn't been easy, but thank you for taking this on. I can see a difference in Ben and Dara because of your mentorship, and you have made my life a lot easier."

I do not thank people very often, but when I do, I try to make it count. I try to make it a conversation that is distinct from other conversations we've had so that they remember it. I would hope that when they think about the times we worked together—years later—the moments that I expressed my appreciation or admiration would be what they remember.

I have also been thanked, and many of those times are memorable. Surprisingly, the most meaningful thanks were not from my supervisors, but from people who reported to me. As I have mentioned, I have no specific training as a manager, so have felt that I have been learning on the job. Thus, receiving acknowledgment from the people who I am attempting to help, guide, mentor, and keep happy and productive is quite meaningful. I received one particularly rewarding note from a direct report as part of an assignment she had for a Dale Carnegie class. My colleague was asked to write a note of appreciation to someone who made a difference in her life, and she wrote to me. In other cases, summer interns I worked with have written notes of thanks (sometimes years after the internship), and I have even received thank you notes from people leaving for other jobs.

Never make the mistake of thinking that a "thank you" is not needed (at least occasionally) just for someone doing their job. Gratitude costs nothing. An acknowledgment of good work doesn't cheapen the work; it improves morale.

RULE 14: Do not talk about one subordinate to another. Ideally, do not talk about colleagues behind their backs. That said, there are legitimate times when you need to figure out the best way to present information up the line. In those cases, you do need discrete conversations out of earshot of the bosses.

Gossip is rife within organizations. Who said what to whom? Who is dating whom? Who does not deserve some recognition they received? You are among the same people all day, and it is difficult not to drift from legitimate discussions of what someone has been doing into gossip. I like to think that my section of the organization tended to have less gossip than average, but that might be because I was not hooked into the grapevine.

At one point, a new president of the organization had rules for behavior posted in all meeting rooms. They were there because he and others perceived a problem with gossip in the organization, which was probably true as we had just come out of a difficult period that saw massive layoffs, an effort to unionize, and the likely dissolution of the company. I don't remember all the rules, but the first one was something like "If you don't say it IN the room, don't say it OUTSIDE the room." In other words, do not talk about people behind their backs. This rule applies beyond stopping gossip among colleagues; it also promotes straightforward conversations with management. Encouraging everyone to address issues directly where they can be properly managed helps prevent misunderstandings and ensures transparency.

As a manager, you *must not gossip*. Whether deserved or not, a manager's words carry more weight than those of non-management employees, making this rule even more important.

It is especially tempting to talk about another employee when giving someone an example of good or bad behavior or when relating an anecdote as part of career guidance or general mentoring. Even if you attempt to hide the identity of the employee in the anecdote, it might be easy for people to figure it out (depending on the size of the organization or the details of the anecdote, of course).

The only time an employee should be discussed would be with that employee's direct manager if the discussion benefits the employee in some way—for example, for purposes of mentoring, career guidance, or professional development. Also, of course, discussion is appropriate if the manager needs guidance on how to deal with a personnel matter regarding the employee. However, one should not discuss one employee with another—*never*—nor should you discuss an employee with a manager who isn't their direct manager or in the management line (again, only if the discussion is for the benefit of the employee). Also, I never discussed one middle manager with another, as that falls into the same category of "must not do."

This rule has a key exception: higher-level leadership. As I've written elsewhere, employees', and sometimes managers', direct communication with higher-level leadership is relatively scarce. Each interaction is more highly weighed because it has an outsized influence on the leader's impression of the employee or manager. One must plan for these interactions. I don't mean that you should lie or hide uncomfortable truths. However, these interactions cannot be treated cavalierly either. There are many ways to legitimately and accurately present information, and one should know why one is presenting information in a particular way (i.e., their rationale) whenever interacting with their manager or higher-level management.

Talking with others is an important part of establishing a clear rationale. Thus, it is generally fine to discuss the bosses behind their backs. (Sorry, bosses.) It is fine to think about their preferences, likely attitudes toward the topic you will be discussing, the goals that they have (vs yours), and the knowledge they have about the topic. In other words, it is fine to strategize about the bosses, whether formally or through informal discussions among your fellow managers or employees in your group.

One example of such conversations happened during the review of a promotion case. During the first review of the case, the director said that he was not impressed with the employee's work nor convinced that the person was capable of working at a senior-scientist level (similar to a tenure review in an academic department). I took this feedback to the employee and his manager. Together, we considered the viewpoint of the manager and what he meant by "not capable of working at a senior-scientist level." We discussed the director's background as a researcher and manager, recent statements he had made at meetings about others' work, and why it was not a good idea to ask the director straight out what he meant. We concluded that he tended to value an ability to work independently as well as in a team. With that lens, we realized that the initial promotion documents presented the scientist's work as being largely supportive of other people's projects. The employee and manager then revised the promotion materials to emphasize how he pursued his own independent research agenda within the context of others' projects, demonstrated by the many publications he produced distinct from those projects.

This approach to the promotion case was much more compelling, and ultimately successful. However, it involved some strategizing about the manager along with his attitudes and beliefs. In other words, we spent a fair bit of time talking about the director behind his back.

Questions About Trust

1. In what ways have informal get-togethers with your team or fellow managers helped you in handling difficult management issues? Can you think of a time when maintaining regular informal communications significantly altered the course of a project or a working relationship? What was the outcome?

2. Reflect on your approach to thanking team members. How do you ensure that your expressions of gratitude are both sincere and impactful? Imagine a situation in which you thank one colleague in a way that is meaningful to them.

3. Think about a situation in which you worked on a project with members of your group. How did "getting your hands dirty" help build trust between you and your group? How did the experience, and the trust built, allow you to navigate future management issues with these employees?

SECTION IV: MANAGEMENT BASICS

The rules in the previous sections represent surprises for me and other reluctant managers whom I have spoken to. Through the rules, I hope that other new reluctant managers will save time, not fumbling as much as I did, and hopefully making fewer consequential mistakes. For example, before becoming a manager, I had no concept of the range of different types of crises I would face and so I did not have responsive strategies. I did not realize how long persuasion can take nor how to go about convincing someone of a new idea. I did not recognize the value of trust—between you and your peers as well as between you and the people in your group—and that trust can be built deliberately.

On the other hand, the rules in this section represent aspects of management that are commonly known: decision-making, delegation, and dealing with change. And because they were well known to me, they were a source of anxiety. These were the elements of management that I worried the most about when I first contemplated accepting a manager role. The rules in this section will keep your anxiety level down (Am I doing the right thing? I feel so overwhelmed!) and help you present a calm and confident demeanor.

RULE 15: You will make mistakes. You must still make decisions. If they are wrong, deal with it and do better next time.

When I first contemplated management, I was uncertain. As a manager, you have to make decisions that can affect people's lives, their happiness at work, the direction your group takes, and the resources available to the group. I feared being paralyzed by indecision, stuck trying to weigh every option to make the perfect choice. Life as a manager seemed awful; I imagined the weight of those decisions bearing down on me both inside and outside of work. I remember asking my former boss, "How do you know that you're making the right decisions?"

His answer was simple: "You don't. You *will* make mistakes."

Surprisingly, those statements did more to alleviate my concerns about becoming a manager than anything else. Before, every time I saw managers make decisions, they seemed so firm and sure about it. I didn't think I could be like that. Once I became a manager, instead of concentrating on making the perfect decision, I focused on understanding the quality of the decision after I made it and what I could do to alter the outcomes or make a different decision next time.

Of course, I understood that this rule isn't a license to churn your decisions. I didn't make one decision, then if I didn't like it, make another one immediately. Most decisions, I let play out for a while, observing how they were working.

For example, if someone wanted to be a manager, I would find an opportunity for them to manage. It might take a while for that opportunity to arise, but eventually, it would. If that person turned out to be a bad manager or didn't like managing, I wouldn't just remove them from their role as a manager (unless something truly horrific was happening). Instead, I watched the situation, spoke with the person about their experience, and sometimes got a sense of how the staff felt about reporting to this new manager. If it truly wasn't working out, the next chance I had, I would move the person from the managerial role.

Even when there were personnel conflicts, I would use one of the other rules to coach either the manager, employee, or both about the situation. But if the reporting structure truly wasn't working, I wasn't afraid of reversing my decision.

Some managers are overly committed to their decisions. Once they make a decision, they stick with it and don't want to discuss it, moving on regardless of the consequences. I never liked that approach. I always knew *why* I made a decision, but I was always open to changing my mind if I got new information. I wouldn't waffle between options: I would let things play out for a while and collect more information. If my rationale turned out to be based on faulty information, I was okay with changing my mind. Even for the new decision, I would have a rationale.

You must have a rationale for your decisions. Even if you make a decision that you later determine to be wrong or that people question, you have your rationale and can explain it. Some of these rules that you are reading now represent my rationale for various decisions I made. For example, my suggestion to "think about what both the new manager and employee could gain from a new reporting structure" comes from my thinking about alternative ways to reorganize my group so that I would give people management opportunities and not have too many people reporting directly to me.

You must recognize that there are different types of decisions and, considering the time spent on decisions, choose your battles.

Some types of decision-making are not consequential; they do not radically affect people's lives. You do not need to spend too long on these decisions, but you do need to know why you are making them. You do need to make the decision, even if there is no way of knowing if the decision was correct.

Spend time on decisions that cannot be revisited and have long-term consequences for someone. For example, considerable time and effort should be taken if you must lay off or furlough people. There are no good decisions in that case (outside of obvious performance problems, but that should have been dealt with at some earlier time). But how do you make a decision that will have such devastating consequences for someone?

Take the time necessary, but even more importantly, know *why* you are making the decisions that you make. Be very clear about the motivation and rationale for the decision. Be sure that you will be able to explain the reasons for your decision to someone else who might legitimately need to know (for example, in the case of layoffs, your manager and other higher-level managers).

Overall, I made many decisions as a manager, some very consequential. I strove to be clear in my rationale for each decision, to myself and to others.

I made mistakes, but I also corrected mistakes and learned from them.

RULE 16: Always show respect towards others. It is possible to respectfully disagree, to be respectful when delivering bad news, to ask for extra work from people respectfully; in other words, strive to be respectful in your interactions with everyone.

While this advice seems obvious, it's often ignored. Today, social media feels like an ideas battleground with no holds barred and no quarter given. Issues appear black and white, and some people completely disengage from those with opposing views. This you-vs.-me attitude sometimes invades the workplace, where people avoid difficult discussions or fail to listen to others.

I am not suggesting the workplace should be entirely calm, where differences are always resolved through reason and evidence. (Wouldn't that be nice?) Instead, aim to foster an attitude of respect in yourself. Encourage this attitude within your team. A respectful culture builds trust; recognizing and praising respectful behavior helps build this culture.

For instance, one of the most brilliant and highly organized scientists in my group, Maya, expressed concerns about feeling overwhelmed. Maya often took on many projects, both her own and helping on others' projects, that had her working near her capacity. However, as a senior staff member, she was responsible for her own time management and setting her own priorities. Most of the time she was successful with this, and I could have brushed off these difficulties with a statement to that effect.

Nevertheless, I sat down with her to discuss what specific projects were causing the most stress. We re-prioritized her workload together and found ways to support her better. This not only helped Maya manage her tasks but also showed her that her well-being was important to me, fostering mutual respect. The approach also modeled strategies for time management.

I've noticed, even in myself, that managers can fall into an attitude lacking respect toward the people who report to them. Managers often have more information—not because they are more deserving, but due to their role. Thus, managers might know about opportunities and strategies being pursued elsewhere, which can lead them to dismiss employees' concerns. For example, early in my time as a manager, my director used to have only good things to say about a particular employee's performance, but he told me these compliments in confidence. When the employee expressed concerns about their upcoming promotion, I was somewhat dismissive, much to the annoyance of the employee, because I had information they didn't have.

In another case, I handled the situation better.

When I directed a group that regularly recruited people for a type of focus group, I developed some new software to support our processes. I was excited about how much easier it would make their work, but the team was skeptical. Instead of getting annoyed, I met with team members, sometimes individually, to understand their work challenges and to adapt the software to meet those needs. For the next version of the software, they were not only more comfortable with it but also appreciated that I took the time to guide them through the change.

Managers must keep their employees' perspectives in mind. Understand that complaints and concerns reflect those employees' realities and experiences. In other words, be respectful.

At the same time, avoid the tendency to shun conflict at all costs. People may fear speaking up in meetings or hesitate to challenge someone's passion for an idea. I have fallen into that trap myself, but keeping things calm should not mean compliance or complicity. The term *managerial courage* exists because sometimes managers must say or do difficult things because those actions are right. However, these difficult tasks—whether it is admonishing a senior scientist for poor work tracking, giving constructive negative feedback, or confronting an employee over a schedule that does not overlap with anyone else's—must be done respectfully.

RULE 17: Try to delegate some small tasks to externalize your memory. That way, you do not have to remember all those thousands of little things to do.

Management can feel like death by a thousand cuts. There are many things—both big and small—that demand your attention or should have your attention if you only had a little bit more time. How does one keep track of it all?

First, you do not. Yes, there are various Franklin planners, Todo apps, and other methods for keeping everything organized and prioritized. Those devices work to an extent—and to the extent that they help you to keep priorities in mind, that is great. I have never been able to stick with one of those systems for very long; I kept feeling as if I were constantly looking for items so that nothing would fall through the cracks, but the search and obsession with those items overwhelmed my ability to complete them.

Instead, I would try to organize my life so that the important items would not be forgotten. Anything else that I would forget I would apologize for (see Rule 15: You *will* make mistakes).

One way I successfully reduced the number of action items I needed to attend to involved how I handled my email inbox. Like many people's, my inbox was a constantly growing amoeba. Although I would occasionally curate (i.e., delete) unnecessary emails—mostly because the latest email contained the thread of earlier emails—I did not spend a great deal of time doing a good job of this (obviously). I used to organize the emails into folders, but that took too much time. Instead, I took the following approach, which has gained in popularity as search functions are enhanced by AI:

- *Used the search function.* I never organized my inbox, except to put everything into a time-based folder (e.g., last six months). Even in the morass of emails, I could usually remember enough about an email to find it within a few minutes. I would use some combination of who it came from, who it was sent to (besides me), keywords in the subject or body, and whether it contained an attachment (e.g., by using the *has attachment* filter of the email search function).
- *Used the inbox as file storage.* Unless there was an obvious place to put an email attachment, and there were several files that needed to go there, I would keep needed attachments in the inbox. I would search for them as I would search for any email.

These two strategies kept me from ever having to search manually through email folders or file folders, or from having to spend time organizing. I delegated my memory of where things were located to modern search algorithms, which have become even easier to use in recent years.

Keep in mind that this system does require you to pay close attention to emails that truly demand your attention—i.e., something time urgent, from your boss, or from someone in your group that requires an action.

To deal with death by a thousand cuts, several admins and I developed a simple system: We would meet once or twice a week to discuss an organized list of things to do, both short-term activities and long-term projects. These projects were activities that would require organization, scheduling, or resources. They would tend to extend over several weeks, while the short-term activities were more like to-do items that would be settled that week or soon after. Importantly, when discussing an activity, the person helping me would prompt me a lot: "What else is there?" "Is that the only activity?" "To accomplish that activity, what else would you need to do?" "Is there a deadline on that?" They would also suggest other activities or deadlines, or ways to keep track, such as by creating blocks of time on my calendar to get certain activities done.

As the weeks went on, we would remove items that didn't seem to be getting done, keeping the list down to about a page and a half. These meetings, and that list, were the main way that I relied on someone else to help me—i.e., that I truly delegated work. Because I knew these meetings were regular, I never had to think about them or the topics outside of those meetings. Instead, I could focus on my longer-term work and the related activities of being a manager.

RULE 18: Delegation should benefit others, providing opportunities for growth. However, some tasks should never be delegated. Delegate strategically.

One of the trite management sayings is that delegation is the key to success. However, effective delegation is not as simple as telling an employee to do something that you would rather not do. Also, there are some activities that should not be delegated.

I have always seen delegation not so much as assigning someone my work so that I can get more done or so I don't have to do it (i.e., avoid something I don't like) but rather as asking for and receiving help. The person is doing me a favor. As I scientist, much of the delegation I did was to find a willing collaborator on work—not really delegation.

But as a manager, the delegation had to be more strategic. If I'm asked to sit on a committee, to provide input into corporate strategy, to speak at a conference (although I rarely delegate those), or to contribute to a paper or proposal, I often ask, "Who in my group would benefit from this opportunity?" That is, how could I use this opportunity to help the professional development or career advancement (i.e., via visibility) of someone in my group? As a manager, a variety of opportunities come your way—you are asked to do things, you hear of people looking for help, and you hear of issues facing people in other parts of the organization. Some of these opportunities are directed at you and some you just hear about. However, if you have an idea of the types of opportunities that would be useful to each of your mentees—the people in your group—you can direct the opportunities to the correct people, which is a type of delegation.

The core functions of being a manager of scientists and engineers—e.g., mentoring—should never be delegated. There will be times when someone who reports to you can get a specific type of guidance or actual training from someone else. But that's using a resource, not delegating. A person who reports to you might find someone else to act as their mentor, which is perfectly appropriate. However, even in that case, you have not delegated the responsibility for the employee's career guidance or other forms of mentoring. You are still responsible for ensuring the employee is engaged, productive, and heading in a good direction that will help their career. You are still their manager even if they are getting guidance and input from someone else.

A theme in all my writing about management is that it's all about the employees. I never sought to be a manager and rarely thought about my career advancement. I was serving in a role that I had some talent (but little training) for. I saw myself as a catalyst for others' work and productivity. My function was to think up and implement activities that would help the group (and the individual members) contribute well to the function of the R&D division but to do so in a way that led to career advancement; professional development; and overall engagement, motivation, and happiness of the individuals. My role was to put others' needs ahead of my own.

RULE 19: When deciding on a management structure, group people by their career trajectory, not their assignments.

The trend nowadays is towards cross-functional teams. Such an approach makes sense for achieving goals—whether business or scientific. It makes sense to have people with different expertise work on projects and even have cross-functional teams that remain intact across projects to develop a sense of unity and smooth workflow. This approach means that the expertise to get something done is likely already in a team. It also means that people with different perspectives contribute to the current project goals, increasing the likelihood of finding good solutions.

For this rule, however, the issue is one of reporting structure, plus all the other functions that a manager should perform. As I have said, there is a wide range of functions a manager serves that are completely for the benefit of the employee—advocacy, mentorship, career guidance, feedback on work, and other related acts of guidance and support. For those functions, the manager puts the employees ahead of him or herself. To be effective, a manager must know about the employees' work and have some measure of expertise in that area—e.g., the manager of scientists has conducted research (even if not in the same specialty) or the manager of software engineers or UX designers has worked in a technology field. Obviously, at some point up the hierarchy, this cannot happen (a VP could not have all the expertise of the folks who indirectly report up to him or her), but it should be true for the immediate managers of non-managerial staff at least.

Thus, although I am all for cross-functional teams—even long-term teams—I am also a fan of the matrix structure. That is, you are part of a team and accountable to that team. However, your manager, who is the source of career guidance, mentorship, help with difficulties, and related activities, should be a senior person in your field who is not necessarily part of your team (and preferably not so that the needs of the team don't get in the way of the needs of the employee).

Even beyond when cross-functional teams exist, or are not long term, I still advocate, for example, to put scientists with scientists, people who work on operations with others who work on operations, and programmers with programmers. That way, organizationally, they get both strategic (career) and tactical (day-to-day) support from their management even as they work with others across groups.

I recognize that this is a controversial approach and others prefer to organize people managerially around their functional teams. For example, people who tend to work on math cognition are in one group, while people who tend to work on science assessment are in another group. The idea there is that you group people based on the type of (say) research they do so that even if people never directly work together, they can benefit from each other's work. You have a manager that knows related work and so can let people know if someone else conducted research of interest. Or, the managers' group gets together and shares their work, so you get a type of cross-fertilization. Or, people in a group tend to be in nearby offices, so they bump into each other in the hallways, leading to the mystic water cooler chats that lead to business-changing ideas. (Perhaps you can tell from my choice of words that I believe this event, which has taken on mythical proportions of late, to be a myth).

The danger is that, without a manager who works in a similar area, the employee loses out on considerable career and day-to-day guidance. Another programmer is going to sympathize with the frustration of stakeholders changing the requirements and would have strategies for dealing with the situation. Another scientist would be able to provide guidance on what journals to submit a paper to or to advocate confidently about the employee's work at a promotion or general performance review meeting. Another program manager will be able to recommend useful professional development training to a junior program manager. Generic middle managers, managers with expertise in other areas, or managers who are primarily responsible for the cross-functional team's deliverables are not going to be as effective in this type of mentorship and professional development guidance.

However, even though I advocate organizing people by their roles, it is also possible to get benefits from cross-fertilization, such as when a manager needs to learn about another research or technology area to effectively guide an employee or when an employee needs to explain the details of the work to his or her manager. Additionally, the employee will likely learn a bit about the manager's area of expertise, just from the types of conversations they would have in update meetings, for example.

Such an arrangement can be uncomfortable at first but ultimately grows both the manager and employee. I have seen both learning something new about their profession. In turn, both the manager and employee seem better able to interact (or eventually work) with people who have different research specialties than they do. For example, I had a senior scientist—a manager—who had great expertise in user experience (UX). However, that person had never been directly involved in the design of score reports, which communicate the results of an assessment along with the interpretation of the results. When I had the opportunity, I placed an employee with expertise in score report design and research with this manager. That employee didn't have expertise in traditional UX design, although was naturally gifted in that area. Through this manager-employee organizational relationship, both learned about each other's areas and about the potential cross-fertilization that would be beneficial. For example, they would share research papers on their respective expertise with each other. Although such a fruitful exchange could have happened outside of an official manager-employee relationship, this type of organizational structure helped in at least two ways. First, just telling people to interact without a set goal often does not lead anywhere—people are busy with other work. The organizational relationship creates a structure in which the exchange of expertise (knowledge transfer) naturally takes place. Second, the employee did need to be placed in a management structure, so why not place her in a situation that could help both her and the manager? Of course, I never shook up the organization just for the sake of shaking it up. Instead, I planned thoughtfully when opportunities of this sort came along.

Questions About Management Basics

1. As a manager, how do you balance your short-term and long-term goals or projects? What strategies can you use to ensure that you can respond to daily crises without sacrificing longer-term objectives? What people in your area could help support you in this effort?

2. Think about instances where you've seen managers that are decisive yet flexible. Talk to them about how they make decisions and what they do when they learn those decisions were wrong.

3. Observe how different managers in your organization structure their groups. What are the skills and abilities of the people who are managers? Are groups of employees reporting to a manager organized by who they are or what they do (if this is a distinction in your organization)? What are the characteristics of groups in which the managers support the employees?

CONCLUSION: MANAGEMENT AS SERVICE (Rule 20)

Managers play a specific role in an organization. You are not a manager because you are a better employee, a more skilled scientist, or in other ways more worthy than your peers. You are a manager because you are willing and able to *serve* in a management role. Let's make that a concluding rule:

RULE 20: You become a manager because you are willing and able to serve in a management role, not because you are necessarily more worthy of management than your peers.

As a manager, you make it easier for a higher-level manager to keep track of everything going on and to communicate by handling day-to-day activities among your group and between your group and the higher-level manager. You strike a balance between a flat organization and an overly hierarchical one. In a flat organization, everyone reports to a manager who does nothing else. On the one hand, communication is direct (one-to-one from employee to manager; one-to-many from manager to employee with no intermediate levels). On the other hand, no one can be sufficiently expert in enough areas to be an effective mentor to so many people. In an overly hierarchical organization, the possibility of communication breakdown is real because of the layers (think of the game of telephone). There becomes a distance between the employees and even two-to-three levels above. A director or senior director of scientists tries to strike a balance between sufficiently efficient communication and personal knowledge of employees to allow good mentorship (with all that entails, such as advocacy, career guidance, feedback on work).

In addition to this mentorship function, your role as manager is to keep the group running smoothly. Your view is of the group as a whole: what resources should be requested, how to smooth the group's way through corporate procedures, how to communicate the group's work, how to moderate the perceptions of the group throughout the organization or the research field, or what new hires would balance or build the skill set of the group. These are more corporate-related functions compared with the more scientific ones: having a coherent research mission, seeing how well the group is meeting that mission, or ensuring that everyone understands the shared research vision.

Many of the rules also have to do with the function of keeping everything running smoothly: making sure people remain engaged, productive, and motivated; ameliorating difficulties within the group or between group members and others in the organization; moderating (and, yes, sometimes "selling" or "spinning") the impact of corporate changes or requests so that people don't get discouraged or disengaged. As a manager of scientists, you might be the intellectual lead for the group (or not if you have one or more talented and willing senior scientists), setting strategy, but you are also *serving* the interests of the group. You are often (or even always?) putting the needs of the group ahead of your own scientific needs—and sometimes ahead of your own career needs (it helps if you are not the type of person who wants a career in management). The closest analogy I can think of is being an academic department chair. This is typically a temporary assignment, and you are taking on the responsibilities of the day-to-day administrative running of the department on behalf of your faculty colleagues. A difference is that as a manager of scientists in an organization, you might also be a mentor and career guide to the people reporting to you; the other faculty do not typically report directly to the department chair.

That is always how I saw myself as a director: I was in a temporary position. As a senior scientist with a long history at the organization, I was qualified to be a mentor and career guide to more junior (and sometimes senior) scientists. I had worked in the organization for a long time and so had seen a great number of people and how they interacted with others (and what success they did or did not have); I had a broad knowledge base to pull from. I saw myself as playing a specific role in the organization—distinct from a scientist or the more traditional view of a manager (as a boss). This role went beyond just respecting others' expertise. I saw myself as taking on a type of problem-solving that other scientists shouldn't need to do. I was relieving others of a type of work that would distract from their main business of research and development.

At the same time, from being in meetings with other managers and senior leadership, and when interacting with others across the organization, I saw trends, new information, opportunities, and challenges that a scientist would not otherwise know about. I could make sure that the folks in my group knew what was coming down the pike and would have opportunities that they would otherwise not know about (e.g., sitting on committees, presenting their work to leadership, applying their work to more operational or "business" oriented portions of the organization). Part of my role was to be a way for senior management to communicate effectively and a way for my group to communicate their concerns or ideas to upper management. My role was to enact service, to keep my little part of the organization functioning smoothly.

The rules you have read in this book allowed me to recognize crises, personnel issues, or opportunities as instances of situations I had seen before. They gave me a plan to deal with, say, a crisis—or, at least, an outline of a plan that I could tailor to the circumstance. Being able to recognize situations (and realize that few challenges are unique) made me more confident and less reluctant. Recognizing that I might make mistakes, but being certain of the rationale for my decisions and actions, helped me to not second guess myself or put off making a decision. Building from my past experience meant that I could act decisively.

Did I remain a reluctant manager? In many ways, it was a rewarding role. I enjoyed seeing the seeds I planted bear fruit: people who had problems in other groups being more productive and happier in my area, people advancing in their career, and stilted and wary (or even adversarial) professional interactions becoming more natural and pleasant. These successes gave me more confidence overall, just as the rules gave me confidence about how to handle specific situations.

I hope that these rules, and my story, will help other reluctant managers to go from reticence to confidence.

Acknowledgments

There have been many people from whom I've learned about management, but three in particular served as my primary models (whether they knew it or not). Of course, any mistakes in this book—or in my own managerial career—are mine alone.

- The late Tony Cline was my first manager at ETS, more than 35 years ago. A mentor and friend, he showed me a style of leadership I later tried to emulate. He was generous with his time, always supportive, and never sought thanks—only urging me to "pay it forward." I hope this book does just that.
- Rick Tannenbaum gave me my first management role, apparently seeing potential I had successfully hidden from myself.
- Ruby Chan, the love of my life, is an outstanding (and decidedly not reluctant) manager. Many of these rules grew from watching her handle tough situations.

I'm also grateful to Thaine Shetter, Harrison Katz, Diego Zapata, Ben Katz, and Tina Hang for comments and suggestions on earlier drafts. And to my fellow managers and colleagues across several organizations who listened to my questions, offered hard-earned advice, and helped me see that reluctant managers are far from alone.

Finally, my thanks to the staff of Purple Breeze Press, especially Norbert Elliot and Meg Vezzu, for believing in the value of this book and encouraging me all the way to publication.

About the Author

Author photo taken by Ruby Chan.

IRVIN R. KATZ retired from Educational Testing Service (ETS) in 2020, where he was Senior Director of the Cognitive and Technology Sciences Center in Research and Development. Over his thirty-year career, he authored more than eighty publications and spoke at national and international conferences on topics such as educational assessment, digital literacy, software engineering, user experience design, and assessment validity. In addition to his role at ETS, he has held positions at George Mason University, the U.S. Bureau of Labor Statistics, and the U.S. Census Bureau. He and his wife, Ruby, reside in Hopewell, NJ.

www.ingramcontent.com/pod-product-compliance
Lightning Source LLC
Chambersburg PA
CBHW071346290326
41933CB00041B/2763
* 9 7 9 8 9 9 1 8 8 9 5 4 4 *